WALKING:
Poems from My Search for God

by Mary H. Ber

Copyright Mary H. Ber 2016

ISBN 978-0-692-61983-4

Little Prayer

*I give myself over to this transformation
the way the landscape gives itself to light—
softly, gently, warmly growing greener—
the way earth moves from season
into season.*

Contents

On the Path of Christianity

Pentecost	1
November First	2
Wedding High Mass in Tucson	4
Father of the Fourth Day	5
Elegy for the 27 People Killed in Newtown, Connecticut, on 12-15-2012	6
Julian of Norwich	7
Reunion of the convent class of 1957	8
Message	9
Corpus Christi	10
Stone Dream	10
Christmas Prayer	11
What Science Doesn't Know	11
Hunger	12
Nursery Rhyme	13
Good Friday	14
Portrait	15
Woman-Prayer	16
Christmas, 2010	17

On the Paths of Judaism and Shamanism

Theophany	19
Questions	20
Kitchen Cosmology	23
Coming Back	24
from Twelve Conversations with My Darkness	25
Sonnet III	
Sonnet VI	
Sonnet IX	
Sonnet X	
Sonnet XII	

Where I Find Myself	28
A Glimpse	29
Walking the Labyrinth	29
Sonnet for My 70th Birthday	30
Vigil	31
I ask to pray like geese	31
To My Possum	32
What the Animals Taught Me	34
A Thank You	36
Yearning	37
How I Fly	37
Great Spirit	38
Dreams	39
A Memory	40
Time to Move	41
Elegy Prayer	42
To my Husband	42
Grief	43
On the Edge	44
My open heart	45
At	45
In December Solstice	46
A Round of the Day	46
After Cataract Surgeries	47
Awakening in Darkness	48
The distance	49

On the Path of Buddhism

The Commandments	50
Balance	52
Zen Poems	53
Prescriptions	56
Buddhists have more courage	57

On the Path of Sufism

I have walked many paths	59
Choice	60

Who I am	61
Where I've Been Called	61
Prayer can be the firm road	62
Prayer to God, the Helper	63
Shaded pearls	63
A Moment of Majesty	64
Sweetness	65
To the Creator	66
Vibrating	66
Escape	67
The Healer	67
What is the difference	68
Repetitions of God's Name	68
The gate to emptiness	69
Prayer to the Giver of Death	69
Is death the last orgasm	70
Let me die remembering	71
Now	72
May the minutes of my life	72
say, God is Big—	73
"Every tongue glorifies with a different language."	74
The same message surges	75
Hard rain yesterday	76
Prayer	77
So here I am	78
In Meditation	79
Approaching Prayer	80
Morning Prayer	82
Aging Honey	84
prayer on my 72nd birthday	85
My Personal Scripture	86
Eldering	87
Ibrihim	88
Lord of the Worlds	89
On the 18th Anniversary of Your Death	90
After the Opening	90
The Path is Yourself	91
During meditation	91
At four o'clock this morning	92

Introduction

I believe I am everything I have ever been—like a tree with many rings. Each year brings new growth, but the tree continues to nourish itself through all of its rings.

I started out with a strong background in Roman Catholicism. In fact, I became a sister in a religious congregation and spent fifteen years of my life there. When questions about God arose, I left my community, a sad agnostic.

During my marriage of twenty years, I learned about Judaism from my husband, a Holocaust survivor. Although he claimed to be an atheist, he was proud to teach me his ancient and beautiful tradition. I never became a Jew, but I have been much influenced by Judaism's beliefs and practices.

My husband's death brought me back to belief. Then my search began. It took me through Shamanism (including a Feminist interest in Goddess worship) and Zen Buddhism.

Today I call myself a Sufi. Sufism recognizes the deep truth in all traditions, so it is easy for me to draw from all that I have experienced in the many paths I have explored during my seventy-plus years.

In this collection you will find poems that reflect all these traditions—and some that simply express my deep yearning to find and connect with God.

You can just dip in and out of the book. However, there is a pattern to the arrangement. The first section reflects my earliest path, Christianity. After that I touch into Judaism, then Shamanism and Zen

Buddhism. Some of the poems in each of these three sections were written during the times I walked those paths and some, composed during the last few years, come from what I learned there, a form of deep truth that continues to enrich my current path. The last section of the book contains my most recent work—from the Sufi tradition. Poems between sections reflect my walking through transitions.

In addition to chronology, there is a rhythm throughout the entire book, the fluctuation between blissful moments that feel like gifts and difficult moments that test and subsequently strengthen spiritual limbs for walking.

In the last group of poems, many of the English titles are followed by a title in Arabic and its translation. These poems are reflections on some of the Names of God used in Sufi prayers.

I chose the title *Walking* for this book because it is a special metaphor for the way we all search for God. It infers a process, a conscious moving toward God, and is used in many spiritual traditions.

Blessings, all my spiritual sisters and brothers who are reading this book. Blessings on your walking.

On the Path of Christianity

    Pentecost

I've always believed
       by the time wind whistles through my bones
           I will feel nothing.

Now, look!
       Stars hug the earth like fireflies
           as I stretch my fingers into space.

Thoughts thin into the shining cosmos
       and the wind blows
           in the time between heartbeats.

The wind blows
       in spaces between my cells.

I could bubble away like a foaming geyser,
       float away into fragments—a seed pod opened.

What holds me together,
       centers my pieces?

Gravity? Thrust
       of the joyous geyser?
           Peace on the quickening wind?

Veni, Creator!
       Veni, Filius!
           Veni, Sancte Spiritus!

November First

In childhood
Halloween
was summer's end,
a candy harvest
we could reap as fairies,
gypsies, tramps, ghosts,
and other
outlawed species.

That night
we owned the streets,
running from house to house
to fill our sacks,
challenging Time that halted
its cornucopia at witching hour.

Next day,
November First—Winter.
A few late leaves burned yellow as we trudged
through damp and new cold
to a gloomy church,
a forced celebration
for folk we never knew—
All Saints.

Now
I am old enough
to feel Time spin.
Last night I fed the children
from an emptiness
that deepened
as the evening hollowed me.

And I missed them all—
my mothers, fathers, lovers—
as I stood,
a black wick
trapped inside a pumpkin
life has carved with a face
I fear to see.

But this morning
trees flame tall as mystic candles,
and the waves of light around me
call my name.
Saints ride the air,
their joy streaming behind them
like rain shine
that will green the earth next spring—
my saints: beloved fathers, mothers, lovers,
whose lives were songs my lips have learned to sing,
who consecrate the dark bread of this day
and feed me heaven
from eternal fingers.

Tomorrow will be All Souls' Day—
yours and mine.
Honor to those who walk this in-between-land,
this Purgatory no one has defined.
I can't take hold of Saints' hands;
give me yours,
and though we may not always feel like celebrating,
let us walk together for awhile,
scattering tears like autumn seeds, behind us,
sending ahead the prayer of our song.

Wedding High Mass in Tucson

Light the candles
of Sonora's ocotillos.
*Et introibo ad altare Dei.**
I want to marry
under this palo verde,
mounding blossoms thick as butter
over stones shaped like bread.
Give *Gloria* for a million golden chalices
        on the altar of Sonora.
Credo: I believe in breathing in
        fire on the tip of ocotillo,
        holiness of mesquite.
*Sanctus, Sanctus, Sanctus.***
In this moment I marry everything:
        the strutting quail,
           saguaros, wise in centuries of witnessing,
           blue ocean of sky drenching arid earth.
I marry it all.
It becomes my body;
I become its soul.
*Benedictus qui venit in Nomine Domini.****
May blessings rain
        on this great, round whole.
May the lambs of God
        have green enough to graze on
and olive oil
        be used in consecration.
May sons and daughters hold us
        deep in prayer
           *per omnia saecula saeculorum*****
           through all the worlds of worlds.

*I will go unto the altar of God.
**Holy, Holy, Holy
***Blessed is He Who comes in the Name of the Lord.
****Through all the worlds of worlds

Father of the Fourth Day*

I can hear the school bell
sing through the trees like wire.
In they twitter—the children.
I can see their souls perch in their eyes
like swallows on telephone poles.
Father of the Fourth Day,
I with my hands as empty as the wind,
I with a spirit empty as the wind.

*According to the "Book of Genesis," God created birds on the Fourth Day.

Elegy for the 27 People
Killed in Newtown, Connecticut,
on 12-15-2012

What can be deeper than hate—enough to kill
twenty-seven people—eighteen of them
children? Blindness? Sorrow?
Maybe the darkness when all our nation's
holiday lights blink out in stark respect.
Maybe a reach for meaning big enough
to hold it all: hate, blindness, sorrow, dark.

Atrocities like this have come before:
wars, famines. When the World Trade Towers fell,
a holy man I know told me I didn't
understand, told me I must surrender
understanding. When I just cannot
do that, I seek the skies. Planets and stars
refuse to mourn. Christmas meteors
begin their annual stream to Bethlehem.

Julian of Norwich, 1342-1416*

When I was alive,
walled up alone inside my hermit cell,
I don't know who I was writing to—
just glad to be able to put my visions
and my thoughts into written words:
how I'd seen the woman-side of God
and Grace in a nutshell.

I was glad to write my favorite prayer,
All shall be well
and all shall be well
and all manner of thing shall be well,
patting the whole world on the back
the way a mother soothes a colicky child.

I wasn't the only woman who could write
and afford the time to write
and afford the pence for ink,
but we were not many.
Now, as I look with spirit eyes among books
stacked mile after mile on library walls,
I am surprised to see mine is the oldest
name of a woman author in English.

Now that I'm dead
I pass my pen to you,
my writing sisters.
Pick it up.
Pick it up and write!
All will be well.

*Revelations of Divine Love was the first book written in English with a woman's name as author

Reunion:
Convent Class of 1957

One Sunday
I find myself back
in the heart of this black
block of a building—
in the chapel
bright with marble, gilt, and tile.

I remember all the mornings
dark sucked out the colored joy of
stained glass windows
'til the world went black and white:
five hundred black serge habits
swishing soft like ebony waves
under veils and starched white collars,
under lights that glared an artificial day.
Figures rising up from polished benches
sounded like surf on gray and speckled pebbles.

On this Sunday
there are only forty-five of us.
So many older ones have died.
No one else is coming.
We sit on a few worn benches
in the lighted front row section,
voices cracking on the high notes,
half of us still known as "Sisters"—
half
not—
but united in a sadness
as we move
closer to an empty chapel,
knowing
it is time to let go and
to forgive each other.

But before I leave I climb
the worn stairs to the choir loft
where the song was gold.

I remember how the choir director—
such a tiny woman--
pulled melody from between our teeth
like sweet and mystic taffy:
chant that billowed clear and seamless;
Palestrina, rich, polyphonic.
Like a magician, she shifted,
shaped two hundred of our voices
with her hands
then rolled the magic singing
over the choir loft railing
on to those below.
My throat remembers.
My heart remembers too.

    Message

There are things to be done.
Some have been mandated;
some are there if you wish.
Choose among them.

Be at peace;
you have always been
a Good Servant.

Corpus Christi

I am filled
with Divine loneliness,
a void alive in longing.

When friends come,
we share bread
dipped in the honey of
sweet thought
and the relish of truth.

For awhile
it sustains.

Stone Dream

*"I tell you that if these [people] keep silence
the stones will cry out." Jesus (Luke 19:40)*

One heavy night I carried in a thick
canvas sack along some dreaming route
rocks that opened themselves into mouths
when I set them, shifting, on the silent ground.

In Babylon I'd once seen storied bricks
speak out, but never with such a tone
as trembled in the black throats of these stones:
"Oh," they sang out together. "Oh! Oh!"

Revolving stars grew still. Rough waters and harsh
    winds
smoothed into peace. Dark hunters paused a moment,
    stirred
to wonder—such deep harmonies they heard
from the bones of earth.

In this smoky latter day, how can I doubt—
I, who have heard the very stones cry out.

Christmas Prayer

I kneel
beside the pool that is
my deepest self,

afraid of demons from the depths,
angels from the heights,
of being born again
as mother,
patient guardian,
mystic child.

I pray
a circular prayer:
Alleluia
to me
and everyone I touch
and the bending roundness of the world.

What Science Doesn't Know

I sealed the night in a test tube
to prove it void and clear,
condensed it into liquid,
and set it boiling near.

After the light was steamed away—
the new moon, mist, and the stars—
deep in my vial tensed a vibrancy
I wished I could disregard.

Sharp! The stab of a cricket call!
My clear night trembled, and
in a scream of shattered test tube,
clung in crystals to my hand.

Hunger

I

I am ravenous.
If I eat the body of God,
will the taste be sweet enough
to wash away my bitterness?

If I make a broth of God,
will it be thick enough to nourish?
If I suck
the face of God, like a lozenge,
will it soothe
the ulcers in my throat?

I'll never take God peacefully
in church again, a wafer on my tongue.
Deus absconditus. How wise.

Oh, I am ravenous;
I'm starving.
It is good
God hides.

II

God, Who guides
the hungry hummingbird

through silver rain to beads of
nectar small enough for sipping,
draw me through darkness

'til my trembling wings
rest silently, until I grow so small
I can see myself in a drop and know
it is enough,
I am enough.

Nursery Rhyme

Sing a song in silence.
Wander in a net.
Answer all the riddles
before you don't forget.

Steal an honest living.
Place a certain bet.
Answer all the riddles
before you don't forget.

Taste the offered apples
without the least regret.
And answer all the riddles.
Answer all the riddles.

Good Friday *

One thing I know: we live in what we make—
the children, poems, dinners. All demand
our skins and spirits. Into them descend
our futures, our fingerprints and soulmarks.
Gasping for breath in the terrible heart-dark
between the moment a thought takes form and then
leaves with its own life, we convulse, bend
over in what has been called suffering, death.

If this is so—and all of us know it is—
the Maker whose thought sustains our pregnant breath
suffers the same black spasms. And in sad,
lost moments, we don't pray to thank or please,
to placate or cajole. We simply rest
a silent moment in the pain of God.

* first published in *No One's Easy Daughter*

Portrait

I have been Jonah fleeing, with a stomach
that roiled in fear against Divine mandate.
But it swallowed me alive, made me a hermit,
and taught me how to wait.

I have been Job in darkness, on a dunghill,
while friends quoted theories to reverse my fate.
I loved them, so I listened as a Whirlwind
gathered. I knew how to wait.

Now I am Peter, my clouded understanding
fogging my life as I leave both fish and mate
to follow a silent Whirlwind and an ocean
empty as longing or loneliness. I wait

until I become no one religion could
recognize. But I am free. And I am good.

Woman-Prayer

Time comes to me each morning
as a woman-child,
knocking at my eyelids with importunate
sunlight, spreading hope upon the moment
like butter and honey over breakfast bread.
I have been a mother; automatically
I answer such a summons.

As the day and I
pray ourselves toward evening,
I can feel
a rounding in my spine,
knees curling up
to chin 'til I become
a circle closing,
an apple hanging free,
a dewdrop gathering
weight upon young fruit.

And enter darkness,
the great womb
where God, my Mother,
feeds and rocks creation,
where I can touch
my birth and death
and my own mothering
together. Where the shadow of
separate moments
cannot break apart
my loving.

And I can pray,
Our Mother,
Who bakes within us,
give us ourselves
      as bread.

Christmas, 2010

In the longest nights of Solstice, the weatherman
says, "Look for meteor showers." Let's do that.
There's no place better than the Tucson sky.

Here, take my hand and watch; perhaps we'll see
a star that summons us to Bethlehem,
Mecca, Canaan, the tree where Buddha sat,

the golden chain kind Obatala used
to lower himself to earth, the mountain where
Coyote stood to sing the world alive.

Perhaps we'll hear an angel, whose bright song
clears all the cries of pain a wounded people
send through space. Perhaps we'll find a king.

Perhaps we are the angels meant to sing.

On the Paths of Shamanism and Judaism

Theophany

I am a goddess.
Of my bones are made
mountains
and the axis of the earth.
Rivers run so deep in farthest limbs
I have no memory of their making.

What my teeth chew
that I may live
I do not think upon.
What beats in me
or grows in me
or leaves
transformed
was set in motion long
before the stars.

Civilizations rise
upon my skin
and fall again;
and soil shifts over them.
I feel it all vaguely
in half dreams.

Sometimes it seems
I live in my mother's skin
still
and she
in her mother,

and it is all too much to know.

Questions

I

Nu Kua carefully
shaped river mud into the first
sweet humans,
watched them play,
then smiled benevolently.
A lot of work—
but worth it!

Next day
when sun shone hot, and air
hung heavy,
she laid her fragrant head
on satin pillows;
too much labor
coarsened silken hands.
When twilight cooled
the summer world,
she left her sheltered bower,
shed her belt,
dipped it in river mud
and whirled it about
in circles overhead.

The drops became more humans—
not as delicately made
as those cavorting in the crystal river—
fit for something
more like work.
"Ah, well!" she yawned.
"Things can't always be perfect.
Even gods
will make mistakes.
I see I'll have to
try again."

           II
In ancient Africa, they say
kind Obatala, in his loneliness,
fashioned companions:
graceful, perfect men
and women rounded into mothers.

He got so high
on his creation that ten coconuts
of palm wine put him into blissful carelessness.
With eyes unfocused
and his fingers thickened into thumbs,
he fashioned more of his companions;
this time, alas, they came alive
bent low, like trees harsh winds have warped,
twisted as vines,
and slow of speech,
foolish as moths before a dancing flame.

A sober hour later, how he wept,
regret and shame commingling in his tears.
He blessed them tenderly. "I am your special god,"
he said. "Always."

           III
The battle-weary Jews
(and, later, Christians conquering
much of the world)
maintain our painful imperfections are not
the fault of a god. Divinity
is perfect, good, all-loving.
Dark snakes, seductive apples, and
our own greed brought us to this fallen state.

IV
These are three stories. Many more
lie buried in the Great
and Final Mystery. And we fumble
with bright Nu Kua's weariness;
we think with Obatala's thick
brain and articulate
with even thicker tongues.

Must God meet challenges
as we do?
Does God seek
love and beauty
as we do?
And does God ever
make mistakes?

Kitchen Cosmology

Well, why don't we think of the universe
as a great big grapefruit
somehow shaped like an egg?

It's divided into segments, subdivided
into little sacs of flesh and juice
meant to nourish seeds—

all centered around a core
strung to the outer stem that remembers
something: a tree, a god, what we cannot imagine.

Coming Back

I know how Moses felt
coming down from Sinai:
bone-tired,
soul-tired,
lugging those two tablets
heavy with prohibitions.

I just came back
from my own sacred mountain
feeling older than stone,
ready to break
the tablets I've been given
if I cannot find a self
who wants to keep them.

from "Twelve Conversations with My Darkness"

III

Sometimes I think of you as a child
I can coax with candy: "Come out from the dark hole."
And sometimes you seem like a thundercloud—vast as
    the sky,
suffused with green, the color of tornado.

But mostly you escape my picturing:
you are the shadow of a bird's wing
just before the eye blinks
or the fading frost-drop caught by morning.

I try to skim your image from my soul
as a finger pulls water off a clouded window.
The air takes you, thought takes you, and you pass
among the moments of my life like a ghost
I cannot know. When I approach the clear glass,
I see only my face.

VI

You are more than the child within, abandoned,
or the bastard daughter of a bad priest
or the black swan in the white swan's nest,
more than the path to enlightened
choice, more than the frightened
sinner with her pack of undivested
guilt, more than the dark circle of karmic past—
even more than the hero-quest.

You are the stuff of creation, the silky waters
of the waiting fetus, the hunger of a heart
for beauty beyond what it can ever know;
you are an infinite pen point, deep border
between the mystery and the truth of art;
you are the soil of Dante's rose.

IX

My husband liked his chocolate bittersweet.
He'd been tortured
into paradox. Inured
to laughter. All his childhood beaten
out of him. Frightened 'til his footprints
dipped no deeper than a hummingbird's.
Yet he sang his hair silver
and cried when he was happy.

I have come late to his secret,
learned to live on the edge of Solstice.
Half of me slips earlier to sleep each night
as winter cold grips tighter. Half of me
stands earlier to sing the new sun's promise:
every day more light.

X

When I get quiet enough to hear my bones talk,
they reassure: "We are still standing, and we know
all that's happened to you from the moment
your mother and father pulled your spirit into dark
existence. We can feel the pattern stretching back
from the bones of your grandparents. Through our
hollow centers, someone is piping music. Go
about your business grateful. Walk
in rhythm. Do not ask
too many questions. Sweetness will unfold.

Who flies deeper—the comet or the hawk?
If you really need to know, make yourself small;
sit silent awhile in the echoes of our tunnels."

XII

Pain-weavers work in the dark. We take our lessons
from the girl with twelve enchanted swans for brothers,
who silenced herself and set her fingers weaving
    nettles
into shirts. Kingdoms around her rose and crumbled.

Princes loved and abandoned her. Children were born
    and wed.
The west wind carried the cries of her brothers. High
    overhead
they flew with the flock. Below, her hands worked red
blood drops into every shirt they said.

She did not choose her task. It simply came
of having brothers and eyes that could see in the dark,
of knowing her own knack for solitude and the stark
truth about how enchantments are unmade.

Fly low, brothers, as you circle home.
It is morning. I have woven the twelfth poem.

Where I Find Myself

Stones
children threw at me when I was small

And stones
rubbed smooth along Lake Michigan
licked by her wavy tongue until
the colors deepened into stories

Shining stones
I wore in rings

A special stone
my lover handed me one day
without a word

Stones
stones I piled
in dark days on my husband's grave

Walls of graven stone
I built around my castles
and my pain

Round boulders that appeared in dreams
to sing me on my journey

And
the black and purple stone
mountain on the top of the world
where I learned the cosmos is a dragon
breathing dark benevolent reminders
I have once been a star.

A Glimpse

Early evening
early winter—
at first the sky
is the color of a dream I never had;
then it thickens, deepens
into the blue-black eye of a god
where points of living grace
begin to shine.

Walking the Labyrinth

I have been here before,
lost
in this place of twilight patterning.

I am always here,
in step
with friends,
then twisting
away.

There is a labyrinth
in the sky.
I have been there too.

Sonnet for My 70th Birthday

Time rises in the oldest years like bread
dough, yeasted with wisdom and surrender. Here
the tiny moments bubble, richly fed,
flavored with raisin joys and cinnamon tears.

Time rises like a melody recalled
from babyhood and anchored in the bone,
like chanting from a childhood church. And all
adulthood's songs play softer than these tones.

Time rises like a roof until the house,
built modestly, soars like cathedral spires,
points up its Gothic arches and allows
the soul to reach as high as it desires—

until the ceiling opens and bright stairs
climb through the starlight into timeless air.

Vigil

Through the thin, translucent
wings of a small moth
clinging to the screen,
I watch the tenderness of evening
receive my prayer.

Sunset moves through stillness
unbroken by the slightest stir
of cassia and mesquite
beyond my window,
moves through air so holy

I feel it touch me, settle around me
like weightless mother-hands.
Darkness opens
deeper Mystery that takes my prayer.
Small winds begin to stir.

Prayer

I ask to pray like geese, like their subtle sky-dance:
all my strident voices antiphonal,
shifting high command, and
focused earnestly
on that one
invisible
Point.

My Possum

Why
do
you
walk
in
mud
?

Avoiding grass,
quickly passing over
cold concrete—
no spackled print to spare.

Where do you live?
Why do you never hurry
to get there?
Often I see you slowly sidle past,
slip from the walk into flower bed, and merge
into gray-brown shrubs as if your lumpy line—
snout, bulbous body, thin gray tail—your very
shadow was greased, for no twig moves.
You walk
alone—
like me,
always alone.

And why
do you circle the house so close?
For warmth?
I see your paw prints
under the evergreens,
then over my very doorstep,
pausing by
my patio window.

Last night
you stayed so long
I saw
the pink of your nose
quiver.

Have you
questions
too?

What the Animals Told Me

*When I grow still enough,
I hear creation teaching me.
Its voices stir my heart.*

In our shallow creek
small fish said wisely,
"Keep the waters clear."

"Question," urged the possum
in its nightly circles of my garden,
pressing pink
nose against glass door.
"Question.
Do not be afraid to
question."

"Search,"
said the dragonfly.
"Circle and search 'til you find it,
all the while darting,
feinting, dodging the crow.
Spiral your search.
Somewhere another circles,
almost a mirror to your vibrant need.
Meanwhile, the air is hot,
the current's golden.
The wind is your lover.
Ride it into joy."

And one day, as I ate my lunch,
brown sparrow clung to the screen on my kitchen
          window
and cautioned,
"Take small bites.
Each moment's Eucharist
can overwhelm you.
Pilgrim,
take small bites."

This morning
in a muddy moment,
I circled back to fish
to ask how I
can learn to clear my waters
when I saw
visiting gods glide through our little forest,
a doe and spotted fawns.
One turned to me and said,
"Be ready for surprises.
When they come,
look them in the eye."

A Thank You

I want to thank
my Navajo sisters and brothers
for telling their story:
how animals led the people
through the roof of the black First World
then the roof of the blue Second World
then the roof of the yellow Third World
then—finally—
the roof of the Fourth black and white World
into Fifth World.

I have many questions:
What is the color of Fifth World?
Is our wandering here a search
for the roof hole
into Sixth World?
Who will lead us—
a metal insect millions of times
larger than locust?

Despite my foolish questions,
I know your story is true;
I have felt the joy
of locust poking brave head out of murky blue
into the yellow world of sun and corn,
the splendor of wider skies and wings to fly them,
of creatures and colors never dreamt before.

I want to thank
my Navajo sisters and brothers
for telling this story
the way
it happened
to me.

Yearning

I want to know God
as hummingbird knows God,
lifting its wings;

as cherry blossoms rest
in perfect trust
on stem and air.

Confident
as sky
receives the dawn.

How I Fly

Some winter days I fly against the wind;
I am a flock of geese, formatting time and space,
determined to preserve a patterned pace,
cutting the clouds with a wedge of serrated wing.
Other days I let the north winds furl
me like a flag. I'm a hundred flocking thoughts:
a wave of sparrows undulating across
the prairie, a spray of brown, a sudden swirl
of busy feathers.
    Best of all,
the dreamy times I circle as a hawk
on currents serene and clear, caught
between silence of infinite sky and spirals
of sound, suspended in the crystal quality
of nothing I can see.

      Great Spirit,

today I feel ready for ravens.
      After they finish with me,
      bleach my bones in sun;
      soak them in salt sea,
      thrust
      them deep into sulfurous earth.
Clean me.
Clean me.

Dreams

Since five years old,
I have been chased by lions
and tigers ringed with stripes.
Hunter-cats leap fences
as I run, child-prey,
through endless moon-lit prairies,
hide eternally in darkened rooms.

Last night
I heard a crystal voice urge,
Touch.
The center of the tiger paw
feels like velvet.

And I did.

It does.

A Memory

When my love
first sought to enter me,
I flinched
in childish fear,
pushed him back,
tightened my
unbroken entrance.

But he kissed me into trust,
into moist
open longing.
Oh, that kiss became a dark womb,
and it rocked me.
Oh, that kiss became a black cave
dropping crystal;
while I stumbled through its wonders,
he slipped inside me
gently as a sunbeam.

Now I ask
to remember
      every time fear
      makes me narrow,
      tightens all my nerves and tendons—
      new love
      need not
      come in pain.

      Joy can widen my thin lips
      enough
      to take earth like a wafer,
      stretch my short arms into sticks that measure
      the growing of the cosmos.
      Joy can open me—
      melt my terror.

Time to Move

The things we cherish, comfortable chains,
hold us, steady us like ballast. So we think
we must choose between the lullaby of thick
encirclement, with every day the same,
and the uncertainty of silent Dark
that generates black chaos,
meteors crashing to the earth on a frail ark,
bow bent to storm and light eons away.

We must walk naked into nothingness
beyond extremes. Beyond the tortured choice.
Walk on our knees to that next sacred place
where all our words have melted into Voice.

For life is movement, every breath a thrust
into our new reality—and breathe we must.

Elegy Prayer

Given time,
there isn't anything the earth
and rain
can't purify.

So I consign
my mother to the earth. Let it soak
the rage
that pooled between us.
Let sweet rain
rinse our black hearts and spirits clean.
Let peace
seal the tears that passed between us both.
Amen

To My Husband

When you lay dying, I was taken to a mountain
in the middle of the universe. The stars
and planets blinked, shimmered like bright scales
on the pulse of an ebony dragon.
And it whispered about the goodness of creation—
the circles of breath and stillness, of dark and day.
And it promised, "Even death is good." An hourglass
appeared to tell me that your death was certain.

Tonight, when I should like to die myself
and the earth is black with solstice, her frozen skin
immobile, all her secrets locked deep—
I remember the dragon's message, take my dark self
back to the mountain, feel a kind wind
rise, rock me, hold me, love me into guarded sleep.

Grief

Between my obligations
and nothing
lies the boredom
of a February day.

I remember the pain
of sweet September moments—
gold and promise-filled as apples—
reaching my arms to hold the sun,
then rounding them
about my pulsing self.

Which would I choose today
if I could choose—
if I could even feel to choose?

Under my feet
earth throbs in silence
deeper than September heart-pull,
deeper than the winter's darkness.

Black faith pinches me.
In the springtime
I'll take off my shoes.

On the Edge

Flat on my belly,
head lowered, eyes searching,
I reach down into the crevasse
toward the terrible voice,
the strident pain
that is my own.

Take my hand, I cry.
There must be a hand
flailing below,
grasping for something beyond
the air between us.
Here! Take my hand.
It is the closest
I can come to prayer.

         My open heart

meets each moment
like the desert meets rain.

Yields to its carving the washes,
bares its graveled skin
to mist or pounding,
grows its greenery.

                At

        this moment
        thought leaps up,
        and I am candle—
        piercing darkness,
        searching shadows,
        licking at debris.

        Otherwise, I
        am the darkness
        or the halo,
        dense diffusion,
        holding candle,
        wrapped around its gift.

And my life takes on this rhythm:
moments I am candle, moments
        I am not.

In December Solstice

I am hibernating with a comet
in a snow-blocked cave.
Part of me sleeps;
part of me gathers
like the winter darkness—
intensity of waiting, being, making.
I hold out my tongue,
receive the fiery wafer.

And it bakes me like bread,
smelts me like a molten metal.
In the spring
when I rise again,
I will be Light.

A Round of the Day

Morning is a drum of hope
as it speaks:
>heat
>keeps
>sweet
>beats.

Afternoon's a bell of loneliness,
as it tolls:
>stone
>holds
>cold.

Evening is a violin of longing;
hear it hum:
>come,
>come.

After Cataract Surgeries

I was whole before: appendix, tonsils,
gall bladder, ovaries. Now I see through plastic eyes.
Where did my cloudy, used-up bits of flesh
wind up? I'd like to bury them. I need to mourn.

Women who miscarry fetuses—they have a sorrow
bigger than the world. What are two tiny lenses
compared to this? But I feel the loss.
Let this poem be my grieving.

When my husband died, his absence left
holes in my living that needed to be filled.
I built bright shrines beside them,
stood by those shrines for years,

watching my gray dreams calcify
'til they became a monument of stone
that crumbled eventually to earth
and filled those holes.

I need to change again,
develop lenses in my soul
that radiate through my body,
become all-lens, transparent

as window glass, so the light I feel
at the core of me can out-shine
whatever dark the aging years create.
This is my prayer.

Awakening in Darkness

Like a swimmer,
I have popped my head
through liquid thick enough to end my breathing.
Into night—
sweet midnight, black and tolerant,
sky deep and wrinkled
as infinity.

I can dance in darkness,
naked feet
sensitive enough to feel the joy
that surges up like the prairie grass
through soil-black peace.

I have not always known
I could dance in the dark,
feel darkness hold me tender as a mother,
feel it pulse inside—the quick stick of a bridegroom—
feel it rhythm out my life
as I feel it now.

The distance

between hollow
and holy
is an infinite
emptiness—
clean as
the inside
of a soap-bubble,
alive as the
center of a gourd
that expands
when the shell thins.
Expands until seeds,
freed from
ropey filaments
wait.
Wait
for the music-making.

On the Path of Zen Buddhism

The Commandments

Ten

I am the Lord your God.
You shall not have
strange gods before me.

You shall not take the Name
of the Lord your God in vain.

Remember to keep holy
the Sabbath.

Honor your father and your mother.

You shall not kill.

You shall not commit adultery.

You shall not steal.

You shall not bear false witness
against your neighbor.

You shall not covet
your neighbor's wife.

You shall not covet
 your neighbor's goods.

The Commandments

Zen

Nothing knows
the Single-Not-Knowing.

The shine on the dewdrop,
the drowning of the aphid,
two sides of the same poem.

Sunlight is mercy,
midnight is justice.
Worship both.

Planting a garden,
eating the harvest,
saving seeds for spring.

Picking up the apples
earth does not need.

Fitting fingers from the right hand
into the right glove.

Remembering where
the stars belong.

The cardinal sings only
her own song.

Eyes greeting
pledged eyes.

Each day, a fresh rose
on the dining table.

Balance

I sit under skylights
on my meditation cushions
like a Buddha on a lotus
'til the world
stills itself
into bee song,
linden quiver,
finally into wind
where motes dance
beyond my seeing
and I breathe
beyond my knowing.

Then my stomach
signals hunger,
urges movement,
and I balk,
focus prayer
like a sunbeam
on a dewdrop,
reach desire
toward the fleeting
moment's fragrance
like my fingers
grasp at flowers.

I will sit,
I will stay
in the silence
of my center.
Then a lace cloud
laughs itself
across the sun,
cools the air,
and I rise,
kindle flame to boil
my tea.

Zen Poems

Such delicate movement:
falling cherry blossoms,
sunlight sifting through the shadowed branches
over gold forsythia—
like diamonds
caught
in rippling silk.

*

Pineseed
with paper-thin wings,
lines of sepia words
I can almost read.

*

In twilight
blossoms float
stemless.

*

The butterfly dancing
in sun outside my window.
Its shadow inside.

*

After summer solstice—
the first fireflies.

*

When twilight and green leaves
offer a moment of peace—
take it.

    *

A windfall—
brown birds
drift over the roof of my house,
land on the grass like leaves,
then lift themselves
back into autumn trees—
blossoms singing.

    *

Too long
the bee rests immobile,
faintly pulsing
now and then
on the fat, pink begonia.
I think this
would be a good way to die:
resting on a flower,
tasting the last
drop of nectar.

    *

I saw the first leaf of yellow autumn
let go,
fall,
drift comfortably to earth,
silent as it settled.

And I too
let go
in amazed
freedom.

*

How gracious
are the trees
in their leaving.

*

A merging moment:
snow flies up through the water
to meet itself.

*

The day trembles with joy,
balanced
like a dewdrop
on a leaf.

*

If air could be honey—
but still breathable,
I'd say
I'm living on air—
divinity so thick around me
and sweet.

Prescriptions

Grace is communion;
swallow it whole like a wafer.

But Awareness
is a piece of peppermint candy;
suck on it consciously, soulfully—
the sweetness and the sting.
Suck it into nothingness;

then go your way
a little bit stronger.

        Buddhists have more courage

than the rest of us;
we're all in love, but they
present their deepest bows to
The Unfathomable, Incomprehensible, Unknowable.

The rest of us
make Names.
We make them out of words for
animals or mountains, for the
processes of human living (Life and Death).
We make them out of human qualities
our eyes can see—at least in outline or shadow.
Wisdom . . . and Love . . . Compassion . . . Generosity.

We want a Name,
an intimate sound belonging to
the One we long to touch and hold
as if our souls had hands.

Brahma, Allah, Obatalla, Manitou—
we reach out with those Names like
frustrated children, arms too short
to touch the candy jar.

Not one of the Names will do.
Yet all will do.
Because prayer is the reaching. No,
prayer is the impulse for the reaching,
the drop of water rising to be carried to
an Ocean it can't begin to understand.

On the Path of Sufism

I have walked on many paths—

enough to know
the truth of all of them
and the Truth beyond that truth.

Each has many branches. It seems
God loves diversity,
and every person's Guide
is found within.

This branch of Sufi path I walk
may not be yours. My desert path
carries no green growth—only simple song
and a search through darkness.

Pray me on my way, good friend,
as I pray you. My desert, clean and filled
with starlight, yet contains rattlesnakes,
scorpions, and terrible thirst.
Give me Godspeed.

Choice

is walking with eyes open
even when all you see is darkness.

Mostly
not walking to or walking from.
Just walking—

rather than
setting down the bag of stones
you carry
and sitting on it,
stuck
in all the noise of traffic.

Choice is putting one foot
lovingly in front of the other,
trusting the firm ground 'til
at day's end
the sleep that overtakes you
keeps the rhythm of that
Walking.

Who I Am

On this journey
I am the donkey
    plodding along with his burden;
I am the cart,
    imperfectly constructed with
    creaky, complaining wheels;
I am also the driver,
    tired, but pleased to be carrying
    a sacred passenger
    with the jewel of love in her heart.
I am the sacred passenger.
I am also her lover
    who comes from time to time to
    plant a new child inside.
I greet myself with joy.

Where I've Been Called

I've gone where I've been called:
    into the water
        (down through the whale—and out),
    into the desert
        (following the pillar of fire),
    into the earth of myself,
    into the sky of God.
I've walked.
And walked.
I've gone where I've been called.

Prayer is the firm road

under flagging feet,
the heart-song of my walking
or the gently-swinging hammock
of my sleep.
The air of my breath.
The nourishment of my food.

And—yes—
sometimes
my heart lifted up
like an empty cup
as I wait in darkness
for a drop of peace.

Prayer to God, the Helper
(Ya Allah, ya Nasir)

Prayer has been accumulating
like pressure behind a dam,
and when the great gate
rises,
down the water flows,
sweeping away my fear,
my hesitation.

God of all the waters—tears and river torrents—
thank you for this rushing,
cleansing answer.

Shaded pearls, *

my people who have been taken:
father, broken during my childhood;
mother, cheated in life's lottery;
daughter, who lost her sunshine heart;
lover, driving wearily out of this world
into the next; dear friend with body parts
extracted bit by bit by doctors
who are skilled at carving.

I finger their memories
in the growing darkness;
then I lift them through the sorrow of my heart.
I give them to God,
I give them,
and I give them.

*This poem first appeared in *The ElderBook* (Finishing Line Press)

A Moment of Majesty
(Al-Jalal)

Tucson shelters in a ring of mountains,
but her rainstorms have no boundaries.
Black clouds hulk,
climb over the Catalinas,
burst in torrents,
then recede.
Sun stuns moments later.

I laugh at weather forecasts
that talk about patterns
where there are no patterns—
just terrible unsureness in time and space,
endless circling of the possible.

Like God, boundless and calling me
into an infinite walking, no rest
for my efforts. God:
always calling, waiting, opening
skies that hold more suns
than I can count.

Sweetness

Prophets have told me,
"God is 'The Merciful,' 'The Majestic.'"
Sometimes I can feel that.
But I always feel my body when it tells me

all it can understand of The Divine:
God is Sweetness.
Oh, God must be Sweetness. Otherwise,
why would I search so desperately

between bone-building calories in protein,
vitamins in vegetables and fruits.
Poor tongue! It hasn't mind enough
for concepts like "Mercy" and "Majesty."

It keeps licking the world to the core,
searching for Sweetness it can't
reach deep enough to taste,
begging for the Sweetness
with no Name.

To the Creator
(al Mubdi)

That terrible hole,
the void before creation—
it lives in my body now
waiting,
yearning
for a Presence that can still
the shivers of fear I feel.

Creator-God,
hold me, stabilize
my shaking jaw.
Oh, stay the course with me
as You promised.

Vibrating

Deep in my throat
I feel two voices
strong enough to pierce the heavens:

one, a scream,
pointed, sharpened in the rising,

and the other, rich as thunder,
insistent as the dawn,
a prayer.

Escape

Prayer takes me in
the way sea takes a stone,
the way night takes the earth,
the way earth takes the dead.

And I rise wet with wonder,
stunned by sunlight,
roses in my
tendriled hair.

The Healer
(as Shafi)

The Name of God is butter;
    spread it over the hungry tongue.
The Name of God is rain;
    pour it over the heart that is
    desert dry.
The Name of God is a root; send it
    down into bones of
    the ancestors. Watch it
        lovingly hold them,
        heal them,
        turn them into
            Itself.

What Is the difference

between the baby resting sweetly in its cradle
and the one sleeping next to its mother's heart?
The safety of Living Arms.

Ya Muhiy, ya Salaam,
Giver of Life and Peace,
I am an infant in my walking.
Just reborn,
stunned by the swirl
of new winds all around me
and grateful for the Holy Arms
in which my spirit rests.

Repetitions of God's Name—

like waves rolling over
the stone of my heart.
In time,
even granite must yield.

Sometimes I feel like faith
has been washed away.
And all belief in love.
Yet Something
is waiting in the emptiness.

          The gate to emptiness

is prayer.
Entering,
I look for You.
I know You're there
someplace in all this darkness,
but the only thing I find
is tears.

              Prayer to the Giver of Death
              (Ya Mumit)

I lie among my broken bones and taste
the air of freedom.
Tears have washed me silent;
ravens picked my cataracted eyes
away.

Time to dissolve
completely. Time to feel
my soul escape,
fly into nothing.

I can see my friends waving
to me—
some good-by,
some hello,
and some
just
yes.

Is death the last orgasm

you can have—
and the greatest—
or a huge sigh
as the dream-flesh lets you go?

Either way,
there must be a moment's
breathlessness,
perhaps a blankness.

Meet me there,
Beloved of my longing;
speak to me in the first
word of the new language;
render me
whatever quenches thirst.

    Let me die remembering

that gold September afternoon
I stepped down from my commuter train
into Chicago's Union Station
filled with monarchs sidetracked
from their trip to Mexico or California
by air currents in that
steel and concrete tunnel.

In and out they darted,
thousands of them, brief and bright,
like flowers flying—

and we, looking up,
up
into the vast vault overhead,
stopped in our tracks,
every one of us
shocked
and smiling.

Now

into the place of Mystery
beyond all the Names,
the place where Remembrance
is merely a movement of the heart
begging for Mercy
or bowing in wordless surrender
with all the senses sleeping.
Temporarily
at home.

May the minutes of my life

pass like prayer beads
through the fingers of my soul.

Say, *God is Big*—

in English please,
the language rooted in
my heartbeats,
the sounds I've used
to sing my heart-songs
all my life.
Other tongues
I've sampled briefly
don't reach deep enough
to taste my tears:
Spanish, Hebrew, Latin, Arabic—
lovely as bells
on summer mornings,
but distant as midnight stars.

Realms beyond
the senses' boundaries
have no need
of sounds or syllables.

Tongue,
be still
while I remove my shoes.
This is a different country,
and the bush before me
burns in silence.

"Every tongue glorifies
with a different language." *

If every birdsong
is a hymn of praise,
the hoarse cry of the crow
must be as pleasing to its Maker
as the finch's melody.

And so must be the sounds
of those who walk
any of the 124,00 paths
the prophets brought.

I think I need to pray in English
sometimes—maybe always.
That prayer may sound
like crow-song
to the Majesty of God,

but I'll never be a finch.
Perhaps my constant cries
will clear and sweeten crow-caw.
Perhaps that's what
my prayer these days is all about.

*This is a quote of Muhammad's as reported in a hadith by Abdulla ibn Abbas

The same message surges

through all the languages
that move
through the Book of Life.
Read—
in whatever language you know.

Hard rain yesterday,

then sunlight shifting
through clouded shadows.

I sit nameless,
homeless in a living room
my soul has left.

A poem wanders
in and out of prayer.
Years ago
I would have clamped
a rigid mind on it
like the glass inverted
over a hapless cricket,
so I can cast it out.

Now
I let it hop
around the house of me
that finds no peace in prayer.
Its cheerful music comforts me.

I think Rumi
might have understood.

Prayer

that comes and covers
like a moonless night—
so thoroughly that sharp thoughts
and ugly landscapes
can't be seen or felt—
that is my longing.

      So here I am,

in this place I've always known about
since childhood, this spaceless place
where often
time turns into slow-time, fast-time, dream-time,
and I float in it like a bubble
alone,
afraid
that perhaps it will swallow me alive.

I have turned myself inside out.
Do I dare stay here in this darkness,
this country of slow descending that leads
beyond the borders of peaceful exploration?

During recent years
I have learned to pray.
Perhaps
that may save me if
I choose to stay.

In Meditation

Silence of blue moonlight
during winter solstice.

My neighbor's house, its windows
shimmering specks
in an underwater stone.

Day comes thick, translucent. Dark
mesquite outside my window undulates.

Finally. A murmuring, soft voices
of rain. I listen . . . listen . . . almost
hear the message.

Approaching Prayer*

Cool morning air.
Bars of salmon-violet cloud.
Prayer begins again:

silence holding the fullness of the heart,
melting and reforming like clouds.

My hands move over my knees.
Hands know something.
They are writing something
my soul has dictated to my skin:

each of us is an earth
with a single bird to fly around it,
and the birdsong is a call,
      "Where are you, dear heart,
            dear heart,
            dear heart?

My sorrow breaks the air.
It's shattered pieces pierce like glass,
pass through me as I fly.
Where are you, dear heart,
      dear heart,
      dear heart?"

*In a place where gathering sorrows
fall away like shining
nourishing rain.*

*Every morning
I am light enough to stand on lilies,
and by afternoon
I can move out into perfumed air*

*taught by the young hawk
who rises to her calling,
knowing air has subtle forces
real as rock,
and the nest will be there
when it's time for sleep,
and sleep itself
is another kind of soaring.*

* This poem first appeared in *No One's Easy Daughter.*

Morning Prayer

"A key turns in the lock of your fear." *

And something Dark surges through,
roils up past my belly,
sticks tight in my throat,
then seeps gently, almost invisibly,
out of my eyes,
slides down my skin.

I have been sobbing for 10,000 Sundays—
at least it feels like that.
I reassemble my selves
as they slowly dare to uncross the arms
pulled tight over their hearts
and begin to sing
in the warm and secret sunlight.

And the song is *"AllahAllahAllahAllah."* **
It swells in the heart, stretches the heart,
pours out of the body, one sweet cell
after another, like wind pouring through an oak tree,
shaking, shaking the world around.

"Lah-il-lah-hah-il-lah-lah! ***
You are the only Real.
You will kill me with Your Reality.
And I await that death."

When my soul cries out
like that,
the body may answer,
Hush,
you are big as the sky.
Vast,
a universe.
Now you know that,
and the earth is your foot path.
Fall down,
forehead touching the ground.
Make your melodies hover
an inch above your awe.

In this place beyond time
Truth is deeper than Love,
you are thinner than air,
and this moment is longer
than death.

*   This first line is from "Where We Are" by Rumi in *The Essential Rumi* translated by Coleman Barks.

**   Allah is the Arabic word for God. Its literal translation is "The One."

***   Lah-il-lah-hah il-lah-lah can be translated as "There is no god but God" or "There is no Reality but God.

Aging Honey
> I am poured out.
> Psalm 22: 1

I have always been slow. Now I become
translucent, drip like honey
through the hourglass of my day.

Moving slowly, finally justified,
I lap like honey over hot toast, try to
sooth, like honey on a raw throat.

God of bees and flowers,
stings and nectars,
make me thick

enough to nourish; keep me warm
enough to flow, deep and sweet enough
to taste like hope.

       prayer on my 72nd birthday

You are relentless
      rhythmic as sea waves
           polishing stone

i sit silent
      and unmoving
           sensing only
                Your abrasion

how can something
      soft as foam
           smooth the edges
                from my granite

'til it feels
      silken as water

sea on stone
      sea on stone
           sea on stone

My Personal Scripture

Then I heard a Voice say,
"Let the day unfold
like a silk scarf,
like a rosebud,
like a letter from your lover
filled with metaphors
the two of you created,
filled with fragrance
from the pear tree in his garden
and a pledge of more surprises.

A letter you refold,
slip into your heart,
read again at bedtime."

Eldering *
There lives the dearest freshness deep down things
Gerard Manley Hopkins

The deep-down point—I like to think that's where I'm
coming from these days, where I've been headed.
No longer up to my elbows kneading
survival bread

or honoring the hands of the time-clock as if
they policed the only law.
I've done my share of a day's work.
In the bliss of evening now, I talk

to friends, water my garden,
pray into the rising moon,
send messages out to the spirits,
begging forgiveness. Soon

I turn into darkness, the deep
becoming,
an anchor for the light
flung out so far by young ones that
their dreams burn to ashes on re-entry.

I don't mind invisibility. Whoever
seeks my company will find a pair
of seasoned eyes and ears. I know
where the young ones are headed,
being there.

* This poem was first published in *The ElderBook* (Finishing Line Press) and *No One's Easy Daughter*

Ibrihim

arrived early in my dream,
holding a long rose-colored dress
inlaid with silver threads.
It shimmered,
a lamp in twilight.

Yours, he said.

And it fit me perfectly,
lent shine to my skin,
flowed softly over a flawless figure.

*Ibrihim,
I can't keep this—
where would I ever wear it?*

Lord of the Worlds
(Rabbi-l-alamin)

I saw my husband die
at the top of a mountain
with comets clearing his path
through worlds of white stars floating
like lilies on the lake of my tears.

I was there, chanting grief, massaging
his feet as he ascended,
pushing him up with the breath
of my prayer. Now I sit
near the foot of the Tucson mountains,

worlds beneath my feet, the hot,
heaving core of the earth, tunneled
with gila monsters, diamond backs, pack rats,
cities of ants, seasons of green cicadas
in shallow saguaro roots and deeper mesquite.

Above me, monsoon moisture swirls
in a blue sky patched with black
approaching clouds. Invisible energies
tumble the dead wildflowers and brittlebushes
spring has left behind.

Lord of the wheels and worlds, I bow my heart.
It is made of light and flares out of my chest.
I see the worlds like layers of an onion,
like flowers whole in the seed and opening,
like something I have never known that I
already know.

On the 18th Anniversary of Your Death

The mountain you went up decades ago
rises pink before me in twilight. I can see
a soft fog swirling. You climbed into night—
a purple-black fantasia with living stars,
gold eyes of seraphim set in cosmic skin.
I hear the mountain calling, *Death will be
what you saw from the foothills when he left.
Your climb will be simple, and it will be soon.*

Icicles fall from my skin, and flowers bloom
at the tips of each finger. I find a lamp
beaming out of my third eye and my feet
skimming rocks as soft as pillows. On the other
side of the sky are valleys filled with children
we never had and words we never got to say.

After the Opening

I do not fear the moment when the door
clicks open. Years ago I heard that sound
and watched beloved souls fly through and hoped
their journey home came gently. What I fear
lies clear beyond all clarity. Deep beyond
all depth: Pool of Bottomless Being.

Can my soul survive what it desires—
a longing bigger than its own? I struggle
to keep my skin while mere anticipation
burns it off. Light bends me. Knees and forehead
arc to earth. A living silence covers me.
When it lifts, my fear has turned to Light.
And Light to Joy.

The Path Is Yourself

You walk through yourself
to enlightenment
to salvation.
And you are everyone.

During meditation

there came a Wind
out of the heart of the cosmos.
First it blew away my tongue.
Then one ear, one eye,
and many people I called friends.
It whistled through my house,
taking walls I'd made of books and music.

Finally,
it rubbed away the skin I hide behind,
and I can feel my pulse
catch the rhythm of the cosmos
as I sit in emptiness,
within the Great Heart
that holds my own.

At four o'clock this morning

I felt them, angels, the Great Ones, hovering
a sacred moment and preparing
to calibrate the earth with a tuning fork.
Our souls, our skins, and the cells they hold
around themselves vibrated like the instruments
we are as the Great Ones bent their light
like midwives delicately turning babies in the womb.
I felt their touch.
                    And everyone on earth
turning along with me, along with stars
and meteors loosening, falling like dead cells.
I drank some water to steady myself,
pressed tender feet against the trembling earth.

God of our humbled hearts, help us to hear
new music we are part of—and adjust our steps.

Acknowledgments

The poems in this book are the word-songs my soul has sung during the journey of my life—a long parade of poems. But there would not be room enough in all these pages to thank the many people who helped me create my life: my parents, my sisters, my late husband, and my extended family; my convent sisters, especially Mary McNamara, Rose Ann Trzil, Mary Sue Koeppel, Mary May, and Sheila Kloss; the Chicago Chicken Women, especially Linn Bourgeau, Gloria Hernandez, and Linda Delaney; all of my teachers, especially those at Alverno College and the University of Spiritual Healing and Sufism.

Special thanks go to the people who helped me get this book together: my editor, Ishwara Thomas, and readers: Geneve Johnson, Jude Rittenhouse, Jeanne Dursi, Dixie Lee Gilbert, Irma Sheppard, Gerry Tamm, and Jeanie Underwood: graphic design and book layout, Karl Moeller.

www.ingramcontent.com/pod-product-compliance
Lightning Source LLC
Chambersburg PA
CBHW072058290426
44110CB00014B/1737